Peter and the wolf
and other stories

Hannie Truijens

Peter and the wolf page 2

The tiger and the cat page 12

Two cats and one loaf page 20

Nelson

Peter and the wolf

One morning Peter opened the garden gate and walked into the large meadow in front of the house.
There he saw his friend the bird sitting on the branch of a tree.
"Good morning, my little friend," said Peter.
The bird answered him with a lovely song.

The bird left the tree and flew to the lake.
A duck was swimming around in the lake.
The bird and the duck began to quarrel.
"What kind of bird are you?" called the bird from the air.
"You can't even fly."
"What kind of bird are you?" quacked the duck from the lake.
"You can't even swim."

They quarrelled so loudly that they didn't hear the cat come creeping up on them.
"Look out, a cat," shouted Peter.
The bird flew up into a tree.
The duck swam to the middle of the lake and quacked loudly.
The cat rubbed Peter's leg.

Then grandfather came outside.
He was very angry with Peter.
"You mustn't go into the meadow on your own," he said.
"And look, you also left the garden gate open. Have you forgotten the wolf?"
He took Peter home and carefully locked the garden gate.

Just after Peter had gone inside
a big, grey wolf came out of the forest.
The cat ran up into the tree.
The duck came out of the water, quacking loudly.
And that was a big mistake.
The wolf saw the duck, opened up its big mouth and gobbled him up.

Then the wolf stood at the bottom of the tree and looked up.
The bird sat on one branch, the cat on another.
And what did Peter do?
Peter went inside and fetched a long rope.
He wasn't afraid at all.

Peter said to the bird, "Fly round the wolf's head, but make sure he doesn't catch you".
The bird flew round the wolf's head and Peter quickly climbed into the tree.
He made a loop in the rope.
He threw the loop over the wolf's tail and pulled hard.
"I've got you," shouted Peter.

Three hunters walked through the wood.
They saw the wolf's tracks.
"A wolf," they cried.
They began to shoot all around them.
"Why are you shooting?" asked Peter.
The hunters were surprised to see that Peter had already caught the wolf.

Peter climbed out of the tree and grandfather came out of the house.
The wolf was taken away.
Peter walked in front and pulled the wolf along by its tail.
The three hunters walked behind the wolf with their guns held ready.
Grandfather walked behind the hunters.

The cat walked behind grandfather and the bird flew over their heads.
"Quack, quack," said the duck in the wolf's stomach.
In his hurry the wolf had swallowed him alive.

The tiger and the cat

A farmer went to plough his field at the edge of the forest.
His cat came with him.
While the man was ploughing, the cat chased grasshoppers and butterflies in the forest.

A tiger was walking near the edge
of the forest.
He saw the cat from far away.
"That's strange," he said.
"That little animal looks very much like me.
I must go and have a look."
He walked up to the cat.

"Hello, brother," said the tiger to the cat.
"I can see that we belong to the same family.
But why are you so much smaller than me?"
"Oh my master, king of all the animals,"
said the cat.
"You don't know how hard it is for us to
live with man."

"Is someone treating you badly?"
asked the tiger.
"Show me who it is and I will punish him."
The cat took the tiger to the farmer.

"Why have you treated my brother so badly
that he hasn't grown up?" asked the tiger.
"We must have a fight."
"Fine," said the man, "but let me first go home
to get my weapon.
As soon as I am back the fight can begin."

"I am not afraid of your weapon," said the tiger, "I will wait here for you."

"Don't run away and let me walk home for nothing," said the man.

"I think I should tie you to the tree until I come back."

The tiger agreed, and the farmer tied him to the tree with a strong rope.

The farmer went into the forest and cut a big club.
He walked back to the tiger and said, "Here is my weapon."

He beat the tiger as hard as he could.
The tiger roared so loudly that the trees in the forest shook.
The farmer beat the tiger black and blue.

The farmer untied the tiger and chased him into the forest.
"Mind your own business," he said to the tiger. "And whenever you feel like showing off, think of me."
The tiger crept away with his tail between his legs.

When the tiger crept past the cat he said, "Little brother, I think you must be very clever to have lived with that big bully and to have grown as big as you are!"
The cat just smiled and said nothing.

Two cats and one loaf

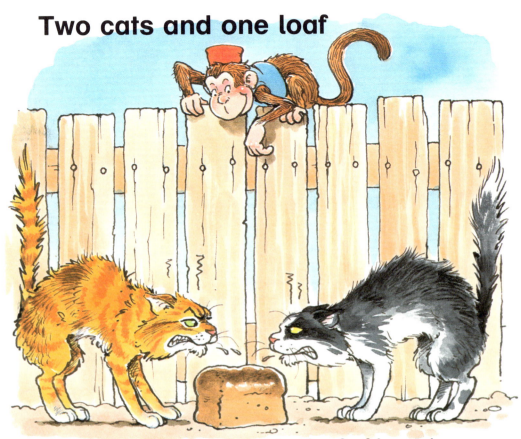

One day two cats found a loaf of bread.
They didn't know how to divide the
loaf into two equal parts.
They started to quarrel about it.
A monkey came past and saw the loaf.
"There's my dinner," he said to himself.

"Can I help you to divide the loaf?" said the monkey to the cats.
"It's very easy, I'll cut it into two equal pieces and we'll weigh them."
The monkey went home to get scales.
Then he began to divide the loaf of bread.

He broke the loaf into two pieces and put them on the scales.
One piece was heavier than the other, so he took a bite out of the heavier piece.
He bit off too much and then the other piece was heavier.

He kept on taking bites out of the two pieces, but one piece always ended up being heavier than the other.

The two pieces of loaf were getting smaller and smaller.

The cats were getting worried.

Soon there would be nearly nothing left of the bread.

"Give us back our bread," said the cats, "and we'll divide it ourselves."

"No," said the monkey, "these last pieces are my reward for the hard work I have done for you."

He gobbled them up.

The cats were sorry that they had quarrelled. And they were also very hungry.